A Note to Pai

DK READERS is a compelling program for beginning readers, designed in conjunction with leading literacy experts, including Dr. Linda Gambrell, Professor of Education at Clemson University. Dr. Gambrell has served as President of the National Reading Conference and the College Reading Association, and has recently been elected to serve as President of the International Reading Association.

Beautiful illustrations and superb full-color photographs combine with engaging, easy-to-read stories to offer a fresh approach to each subject in the series. Each DK READER is guaranteed to capture a child's interest while developing his or her reading skills, general knowledge, and love of reading.

The five levels of DK READERS are aimed at different reading abilities, enabling you to choose the books that are exactly right for your child:

Pre-level 1: Learning to read
Level 1: Beginning to read
Level 2: Beginning to read alone
Level 3: Reading alone
Level 4: Proficient readers

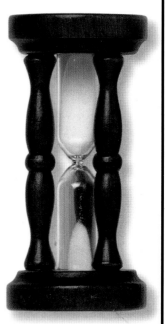

The "normal" age at which a child begins to read can be anywhere from three to eight years old. Adult participation through the lower levels is very helpful for providing encouragement, discussing storylines, and sounding out unfamiliar words.

No matter which level you select, you can be sure that you are helping your child learn to read, then read to learn!

LONDON, NEW YORK, MUNICH,
MELBOURNE, AND DELHI

Series Editor Deborah Lock
Art Editor Sadie Thomas
U.S. Editor John Searcy
DTP Designer Ben Hung
Production Georgina Hayworth
Picture Researcher Rob Nunn
Illustrator Peter Dennis

Reading Consultant
Linda Gambrell, Ph.D.

First American Edition, 2007
07 08 09 10 11 10 9 8 7 6 5 4 3 2 1
Published in the United States by DK Publishing
375 Hudson Street, New York, New York 10014

DK books are available at special discounts when purchased in bulk for
sales promotions, premiums, fund-raising, or educational use.
For details, contact:
DK Publishing Special Markets
375 Hudson Street
New York, New York 10014
SpecialSales@dk.com

A catalog record for this book is available
from the Library of Congress

ISBN: 978-0-7566-2948-9 (Paperback)
ISBN: 978-0-7566-2949-6 (Hardcover)

Color reproduction by Colourscan, Singapore
Printed and bound in China by L. Rex Printing Co. Ltd.

The publisher would like to thank the following for their kind
permission to reproduce their photographs.
a=above, b=below, c=center, l=left, r=right, t=top.
Alamy Images: A Room With Views 6-7; Richard Levine 48br.
The Bridgeman Art Library: The Makins Collection 24. **Corbis:**
22br; Bettmann 26; Grace/zefa 4b. Hulton-Deutsch Collection
19tr; Wolfgang Kaehler 14; Markus Moellenberg/zefa 29t; Carl &
Ann Purcell 21bl; Tim Thompson 3cb, 20r; Holger Winkler/zefa
5c. **DK Images:** NASA 28bl, 28cb; National Maritime Museum,
London 2tr, 19tl; Natural History Museum, London 25tr; Stephen
Oliver 15tl, 30cr, 49br; The Science Museum, London 15tr, 18crb.
National Institute of Standards and Technology / NIST: Geoffrey
Wheeler Photography 28tr. **Science & Society Picture Library:**
Science Museum 13cr, 13cra, 13tr. **Science Photo Library:** 16tl.
SuperStock: Maria Ferrari 16-17.

All other images © Dorling Kindersley Limited
For more information see: www.dkimages.com

Discover more at
www.dk.com

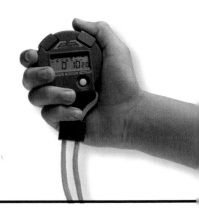

 **READERS**

 BEGINNING TO READ ALONE 2

Telling Time

Written by Patricia J. Murphy

DK Publishing

Do you know what time it is?

We tell time many times a day.

When is soccer practice?

What time is dinner?

*When does
the party start?*

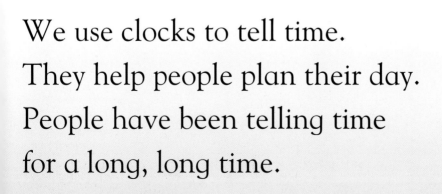

*What time will
you get there?*

We use clocks to tell time.
They help people plan their day.
People have been telling time
for a long, long time.

Clocks from long ago did not look
like ours and they did not keep
the best time either.
This is the story of how clocks
have changed.

Timeline

Prehistoric times

Once upon a time, people woke up when the sun rose and went to bed when the moon and stars came out. These were the first clocks. Sometimes, people used stone pillars to mark the movement of the sun, moon, and stars during the year.

Stonehenge in England

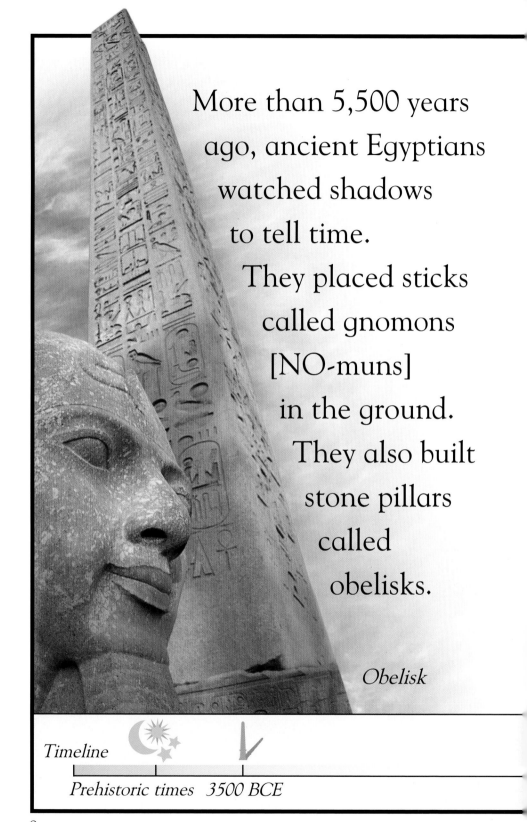

More than 5,500 years ago, ancient Egyptians watched shadows to tell time. They placed sticks called gnomons [NO-muns] in the ground. They also built stone pillars called obelisks.

Obelisk

These sticks and obelisks cast
long shadows on the ground.
As the sun moved, the direction
of the shadows told people
what part of the day it was.
These devices were
the very first sundials.

In 1500 BCE,
the Egyptians built
an even better
sundial.

Timeline

Prehistoric times   3500 BCE   1500 BCE

It was shaped like a T and
had special markings.
The marks split the day into
ten hours of daylight and
two hours of twilight.
Like all sundials, this one could
only tell time in sunlight.
People could not tell what time
it was on cloudy days or at night.

Time for bed, Tut!
Around 600 BCE,
Egyptians lined up
merkhets [MER-kets]
with the stars to tell
the time at night.

Starting in 1400 BCE, ancient Egyptians and Greeks used water clocks to tell time during the day and the night.

Timeline

Prehistoric times   3500 BCE   1500 BCE   1400 BCE

Water-clock tower

In 1088, Su Sung, a Chinese monk, built an amazing water-clock tower. It was more than 30 feet (9 m) tall and had many moving parts.

Water was poured into a bowl with holes in it. As the water dripped out through the holes, people checked the water levels using special marks. This told them how much time had passed.

Water-level marks

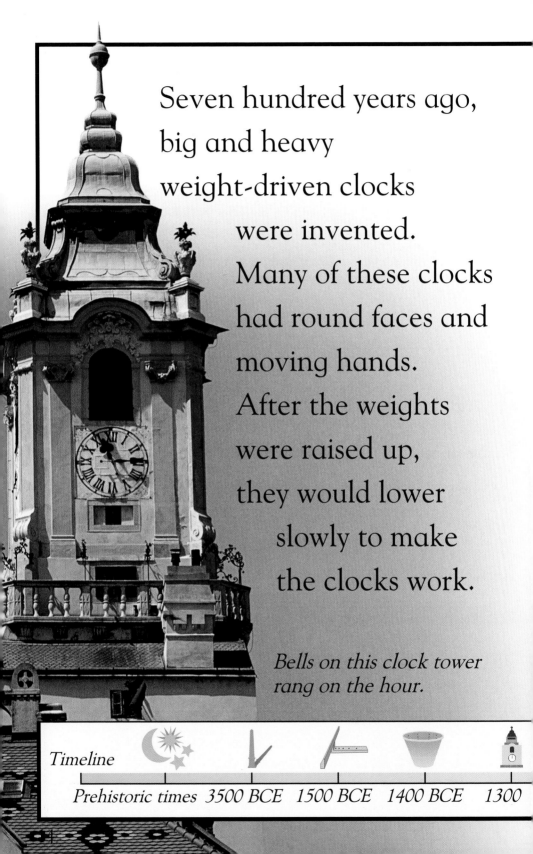

Seven hundred years ago,
big and heavy
weight-driven clocks
were invented.
Many of these clocks
had round faces and
moving hands.
After the weights
were raised up,
they would lower
slowly to make
the clocks work.

Bells on this clock tower rang on the hour.

Timeline

Prehistoric times   3500 BCE   1500 BCE   1400 BCE   1300

The outside and inside of a pocket watch

Two hundred years later, clocks were made that were powered by springs instead of weights. They were small and light, and some were made to fit in pockets. These tiny timepieces were the first pocket watches.

1500

In 1582, Galileo Galilei noticed that an oil lamp swinging from a chain kept perfect time. He found that a swinging weight always took the same number of beats to go backward and forward.

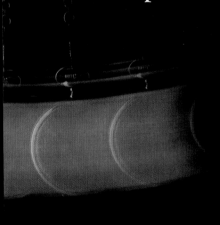

The cuckoo clock

This pendulum clock makes a whistle that sounds like a cuckoo bird every hour. If it is 12 o'clock, it whistles 12 times!

Another name for a swinging weight is a pendulum.

In 1657, Christiaan Huygens invented a clock that used a pendulum to keep time.

pendulum

On the high seas, sailors needed to know the exact time to find their way. Pendulum clocks needed to stand still and would not work on choppy waters.

Sands of time

Sometimes, sailors used hourglasses filled with sand or powdered eggshells to tell time. The powder would take one hour to flow from the top bulb to the bottom bulb.

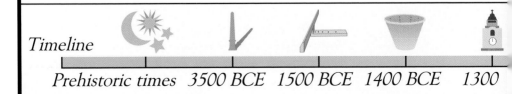

Timeline

Prehistoric times   3500 BCE   1500 BCE   1400 BCE   1300

John Harrison

H4 chronometer

In 1759, John Harrison invented
the H4 chronometer, a special clock
to use on ships.
It worked so well that it won
a prize from the British government.

1500   1657   1759

Clocks had problems on land, too.
Each town set its clocks
using the sun.
When the sun reached
the highest place in
the sky, it was 12 noon
for that town.

Timeline

Prehistoric times   3500 BCE   1500 BCE   1400 BCE   1300

Since the sun reaches the highest
place in the sky at different times
in different places, every town
had its own 12 noon!
Time was different
all over the place.
It was a mess!

Many people thought it was silly for every town to have its own time. They asked questions like: "How can railroads and mail coaches run on time?" "How can people meet for lunch or do business?" "How can we fix this problem?" Sandford Fleming, a railroad worker, knew the answer.

Greenwich Mean Time
Greenwich Mean Time (GMT) is the time in Greenwich, England. Each time zone was described by how many hours away from GMT it was.

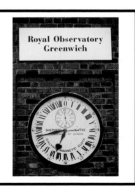

Royal Observatory Greenwich

Timeline

Prehistoric times   3500 BCE   1500 BCE   1400 BCE   1300

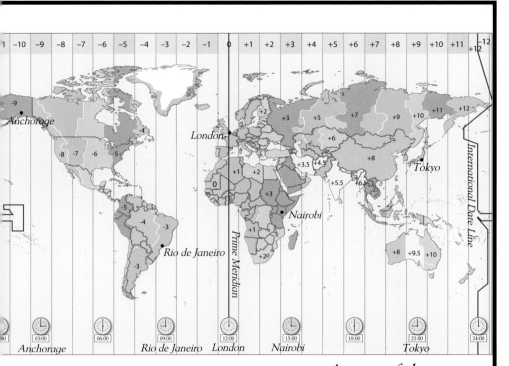

A map of the world's time zones

His idea was to divide the world into 24 time zones. Each zone was exactly one hour apart from its neighbors. Now, time was the same for everyone in each zone.

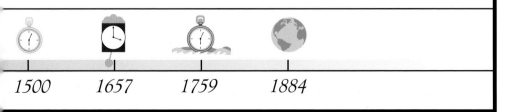

In the 1880s, women were
the first to wear wristwatches.
After soldiers wore them in
World War I, men liked
to wear them as well.

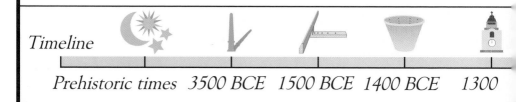

Later, watches with
tiny quartz crystals
inside would become
the best timekeepers.

Quartz crystal

The crystals moved like

Quartz watch

pendulums, but kept
even better time.
Quartz watches are
still popular today.

Digital quartz watches

In 1972, quartz watches
went digital. A display of
numbers appeared instead
of a clock face.

The first
atomic clock

Timeline

Prehistoric times   3500 BCE   1500 BCE   1400 BCE   1300

Quartz watches no longer keep
the most exact time.
What does?
Atomic clocks do!
Atomic clocks use atoms—
tiny particles, too small for us
to see—to help tell time.
The atoms act like pendulums.
They move backward and forward
billions of times per second.
This lets atomic clocks tell time
to a billionth of a second.

*Modern atomic
wristwatch*

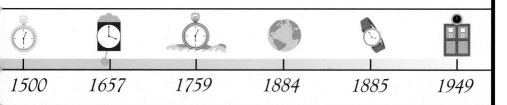

1500   1657   1759   1884   1885   1949

Exact timekeeping

In 1999, scientists invented the world's most exact clock. It is called NIST-F1. It will not gain or lose a second in millions of years.

Space travel

So, why do we need to tell time to a billionth of a second?

Satellites

Radio and television broadcasts

Many forms of
technology that
we use today need
the split-second time
of an atomic clock
to work.

These pages show
just a few examples.

*Cell
phones*

Today, clocks come in all shapes, sizes, colors, and styles. Some flash, make sounds, play music, or say the time out loud. Others time how fast you run.

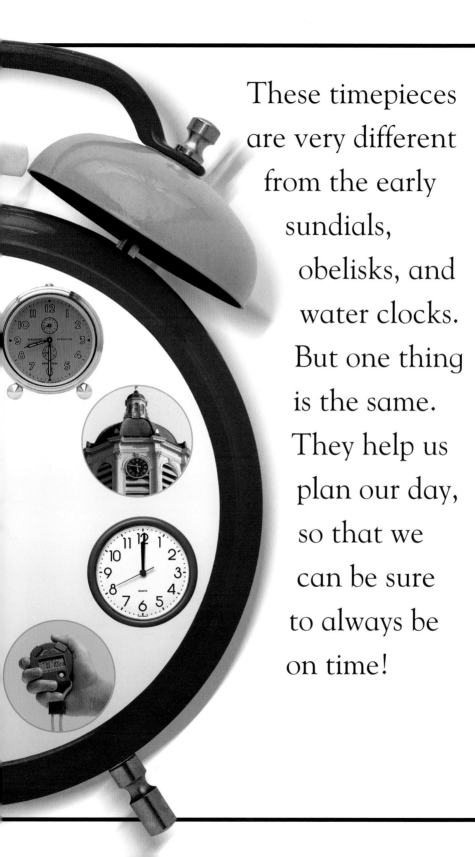

These timepieces are very different from the early sundials, obelisks, and water clocks. But one thing is the same. They help us plan our day, so that we can be sure to always be on time!

Timely facts

Long-case clocks were built to hide their long pendulums. The song "Grandfather's Clock" written in 1876, inspired people to call them grandfather clocks.

The ancient Egyptians were the first people to divide the hour into 60 parts, or minutes. Their number system was based on the number 60, which is easy to divide by 2, 3, 4, 5, and 10.

The world's smallest clock is an atomic clock the size of a grain of rice created by the National Institute for Standards and Technology in Boulder, Colorado, in 2004.

The Colgate Palmolive clock is one of the world's biggest clocks. It measures 55 feet (16.8 m) around! It is located in Jersey City, New Jersey. It was built in 1924.

Colgate